Find more heroes to read about on:
WWW.HEROESOFLIBERTY.COM

Joyce Claiborne-West

Amy Coney Barrett – A Justice and a Mother

Illustrations by Ivana Besevic

Text copyright © Heroes of Liberty Inc., 2021

Illustrations copyright Heroes of Liberty Inc., 2021

1216 Broadway, New York, NY 10001

Heroes of Liberty Inc.
1216 Broadway, New York, NY 10001

Find more heroes to read about on:
WWW.HEROESOFLIBERTY.COM

HEROES
OF
LIBERTY

Amy Coney Barrett

A JUSTICE AND A MOTHER

Amy Coney Barrett

is a justice in the Supreme Court of
the United States. The Supreme
Court is the highest court
in America, and the nine
judges who serve there are
all called justices. The court
sits in a big, white, majestic
building on 1 First Street NE
in Washington, DC.

Amy has a very sharp mind. She
also has a very big heart: she's
the mother of seven children,
two of whom she adopted because
they had no home of their own.

One of the most important skills
in life is to know when to listen to your
head and when to listen to your heart.
Amy's good at this. It's a skill that
helps her to be a good judge—and
to be a good mother too.

BORN – JANUARY 28, 1972
NEW ORLEANS, LOUISIANA

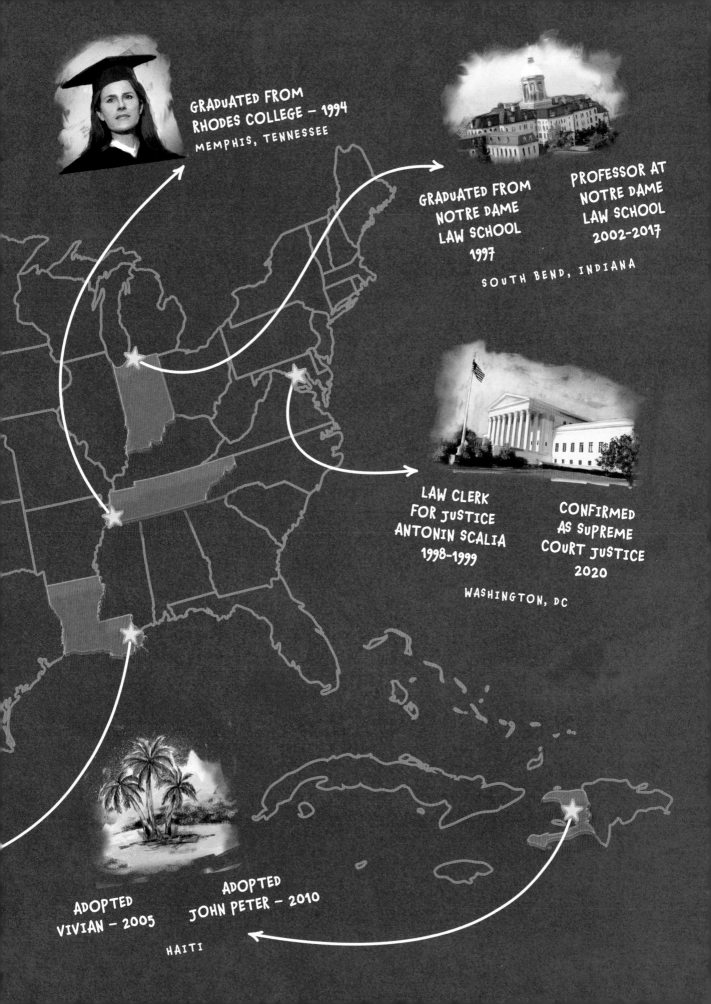

GRADUATED FROM
RHODES COLLEGE – 1994
MEMPHIS, TENNESSEE

GRADUATED FROM
NOTRE DAME
LAW SCHOOL
1997

PROFESSOR AT
NOTRE DAME
LAW SCHOOL
2002-2017

SOUTH BEND, INDIANA

LAW CLERK
FOR JUSTICE
ANTONIN SCALIA
1998-1999

CONFIRMED
AS SUPREME
COURT JUSTICE
2020

WASHINGTON, DC

ADOPTED
VIVIAN – 2005

ADOPTED
JOHN PETER – 2010

HAITI

Amy was born in New Orleans, Louisiana, in 1972. Her father, Michael Coney, was a lawyer. Her mother, Linda, taught French. Michael and Linda wanted a big family. After they had Amy, they went on to have six more children: five girls and one boy. They needed a very big car—a car with nine seats—to drive everyone to church.

But it often wasn't just the nine of them back then. Amy had lots of aunts and uncles, and most of them had big families too. When they all got together, people would stop and stare at the lively crowd. It was such a big crowd that some thought it was a school outing! Amy loved this growing up. She knew that one day she'd want to have lots of children of her own.

Amy went to St. Mary's Dominican High
School, which is a high school just for
girls. She remembers her time there
fondly. She was a very ambitious student
and won lots of prizes for her schoolwork.

With six younger siblings, she had
plenty of work at home too. Being the
oldest, Amy was the first to earn her
driver's license. Her parents bought Amy
a used car so that she could drive her
younger brother and sisters around.

It was a big old 1977 Buick LeSabre. People around town would recognize the big car and know it was Amy passing by. And she passed by a lot. She worked as a babysitter to make extra money, and she'd drive the kids she watched to soccer practice, boy scout meetings, and music class.

All this, apart from shuttling six younger siblings around. Isn't it great to have an older sister with wheels when you need a ride?

Amy decided to study law at the University of Notre Dame, just like her father had. She loved Notre Dame's football team, and she and her friends would cheer for them at home games.

In class, Amy learned about the Constitution. The Constitution is the highest law of the land. It explains what rights we have as citizens and how the American government should work.

The Constitution says that America should have a president, who is also the commander in chief of all of our military forces. We choose the president ourselves in an election every four years.

And if we think that the president isn't doing a good job, we can choose someone else who we think will do better. This is because the Constitution guarantees that we are free and that no one can govern us without our consent.

The Constitution also says that the citizens of every state should choose people to represent them in Washington, DC. These people are called representatives and senators, and together they make up the United States Congress. The Congress is in charge of making laws.

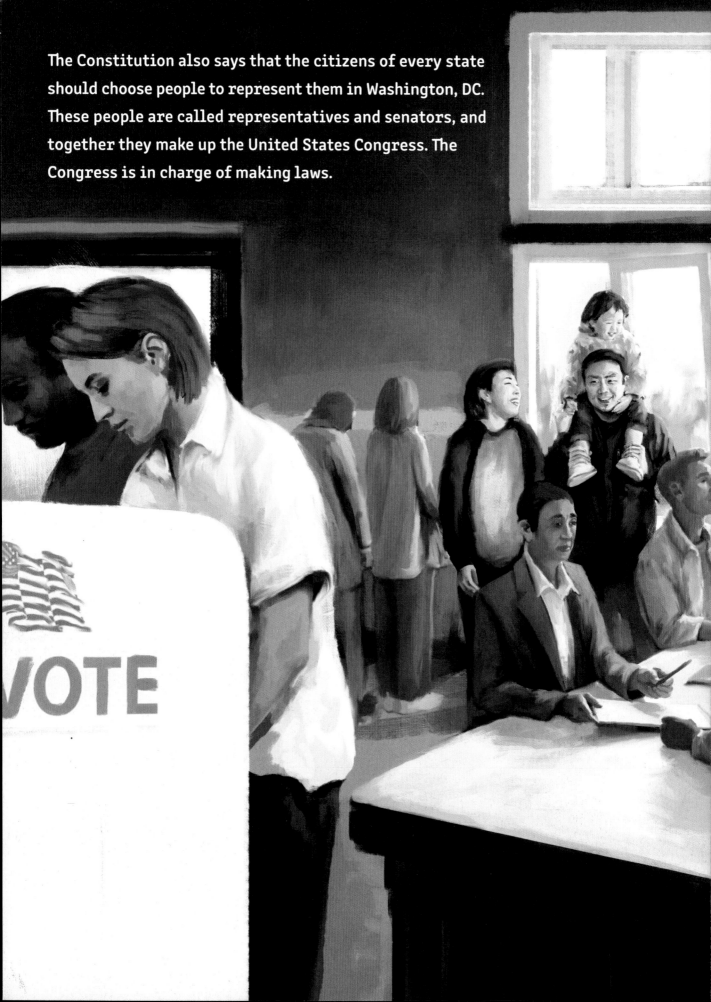

Finally, the Constitution says that we should have a Supreme Court, whose justices also sit in our nation's capital. It's their job to make sure that our laws and our government follow the Constitution.

Although Amy's mind was focused on her studies, her heart was open. Soon a smart, handsome student named Jesse caught her attention, and they fell in love. They talked for hours, they took long walks, and they had lots of nice dinners. Unlike Amy, Jesse was an only child. But like Amy, Jesse, too, wanted to have a big family. They decided to get married and have children of their own.

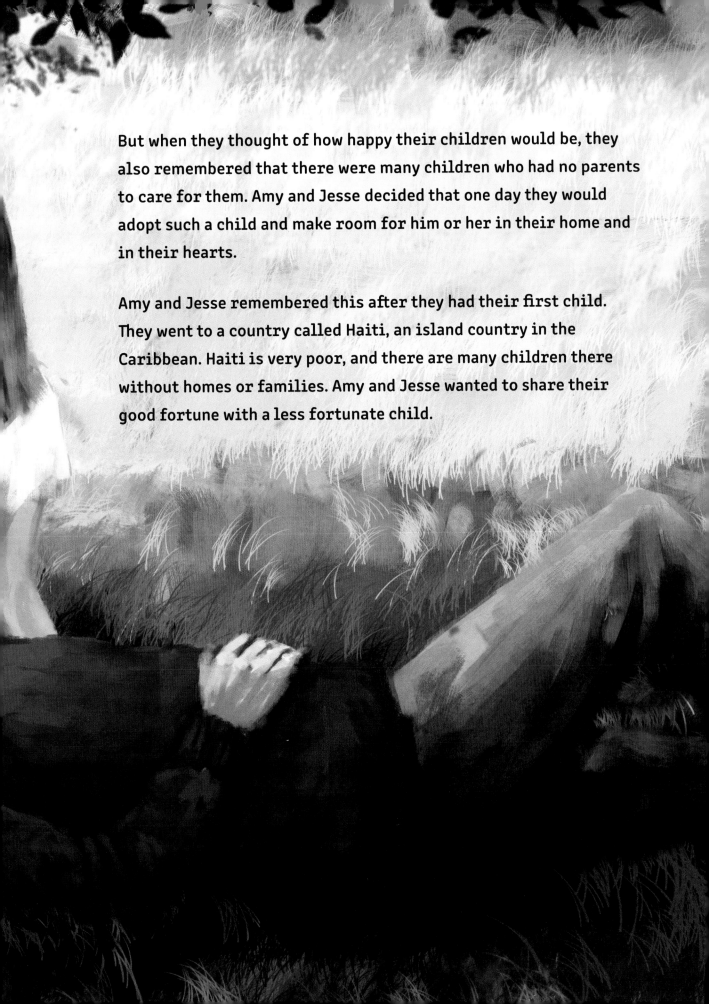

But when they thought of how happy their children would be, they also remembered that there were many children who had no parents to care for them. Amy and Jesse decided that one day they would adopt such a child and make room for him or her in their home and in their hearts.

Amy and Jesse remembered this after they had their first child. They went to a country called Haiti, an island country in the Caribbean. Haiti is very poor, and there are many children there without homes or families. Amy and Jesse wanted to share their good fortune with a less fortunate child.

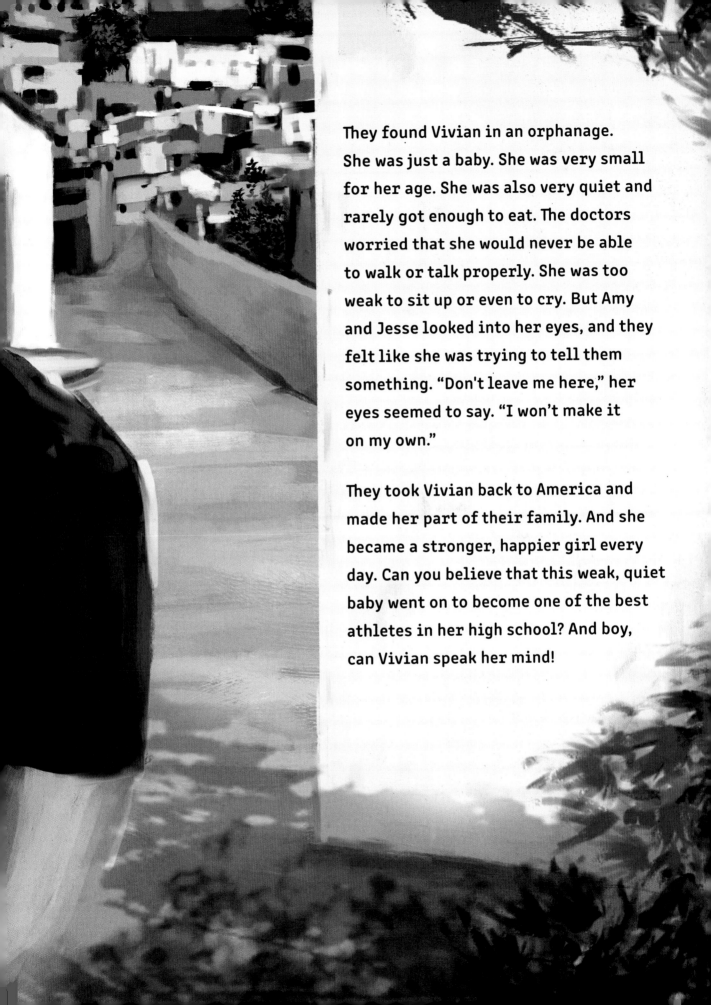

They found Vivian in an orphanage. She was just a baby. She was very small for her age. She was also very quiet and rarely got enough to eat. The doctors worried that she would never be able to walk or talk properly. She was too weak to sit up or even to cry. But Amy and Jesse looked into her eyes, and they felt like she was trying to tell them something. "Don't leave me here," her eyes seemed to say. "I won't make it on my own."

They took Vivian back to America and made her part of their family. And she became a stronger, happier girl every day. Can you believe that this weak, quiet baby went on to become one of the best athletes in her high school? And boy, can Vivian speak her mind!

Year by year, Amy and Jesse's family grew and grew. Amy worked as a law professor at Notre Dame, the same place where she graduated. She still loved going to football games, although now she sat with the other professors rather than jumping, and cheering, and shouting with the students like she used to do.

Jesse worked as a prosecutor for the government, helping put criminals away.

The Barretts had a happy and busy life in their small town of South Bend, Indiana. But they never forgot a boy they met during one of their visits to Haiti. His name was John Peter, and like Vivian, he was an orphan. Amy and Jesse had wanted to bring him home too.

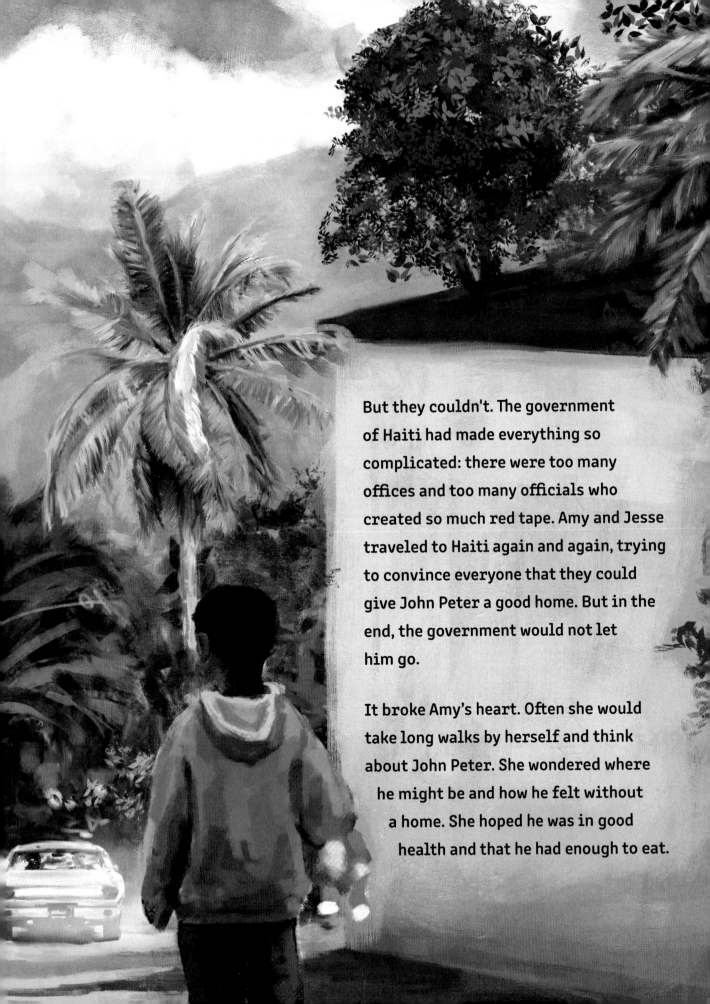

But they couldn't. The government of Haiti had made everything so complicated: there were too many offices and too many officials who created so much red tape. Amy and Jesse traveled to Haiti again and again, trying to convince everyone that they could give John Peter a good home. But in the end, the government would not let him go.

It broke Amy's heart. Often she would take long walks by herself and think about John Peter. She wondered where he might be and how he felt without a home. She hoped he was in good health and that he had enough to eat.

Then one day, there was a huge earthquake in Haiti. It was awful and it devastated the country. Buildings, roads, and bridges were shattered. Many people lost their homes.

Although many Haitian government offices had been destroyed, they managed to work with the American government to save as many children as they could.

Finally, Amy and Jesse received a call. "Do you still want John Peter?" a lady asked. Amy's eyes welled with tears. She couldn't believe what she was hearing. "Of course we do!" she said. "Yes, of course!"

An airplane took John Peter to Florida and Jesse went to meet him there. Then they started their journey together back to South Bend, Indiana, making a stop at Chicago's Midway International Airport. John Peter was shocked when he stepped off the plane in Chicago.

The weather in Haiti is very hot all year round since it's close to the Earth's equator. Can you imagine what John Peter thought when he first saw an airport covered in snow? Can you imagine his surprise when he felt the biting cold of Chicago at Christmas time?

John Peter looked at Jesse in surprise. Jesse
knew what the boy must be thinking. He smiled.
"Oh," he said, "This is not where you're going
to live, little John Peter."

To this day, the Barrett family laughs at the memory of this story. Because the home into which they took John Peter is not cold at all: it is warm and loving. And though South Bend is not as warm as Haiti, it does have nice weather—at least half of the year.

By and by, Amy's family grew. She and Jesse became proud parents of seven children! Her career also took off. She became a federal judge. She was very busy.

She would get up early in the morning
to work quietly at her desk while
everyone else was still asleep.

This way, she
would have time
to spend with her family
later in the day. She especially liked
to bake cakes for her kids' birthdays—all
seven of them, every year. She said she
wanted birthday cakes to always have the
taste of their mother's love. And boy, did she
get good at making fancy cakes!

Amy said the kids thought Jesse's work was cooler because he put criminals in jail. When they caught an arsonist who set fire to people's property in South Bend, the children wanted to hear every last detail. How did the police catch him? How could they prove it was him? How did Jesse convince the jury that the defendant was guilty as charged?

It might have been even cooler if Amy was the judge in the case, but this isn't possible. American courts strive to be fair to everybody, even to criminals.

They give everyone a chance to try and prove his innocence; after all, we want to be sure that we aren't punishing people who did nothing wrong.

So of course, you can't have a prosecutor who is married to the judge, because then, you see, the judge may be inclined to take her husband's side. A judge can't let her heart confuse her head when she sits in court. She needs to listen to everyone with an open mind.

One day, Amy got a call from the president of the United States. He said he had chosen her to sit on the Supreme Court.

Now, you may be surprised to hear that Amy had worked in the United States Supreme Court before. Not as a justice, of course, but as a law clerk. When she finished law school at the top of her class, Amy took this position under a very famous judge: Supreme Court Justice Antonin Scalia.

Justice Scalia believed that our laws should follow the Constitution precisely as its authors—the wise founders of the United States—had originally intended. This is why he was called an "originalist."

Amy liked Justice Scalia a lot. She loved his big rolling laugh and his sense of humor. She also admired him because she, too, was an originalist.

Sadly, the great Justice Scalia had passed away by the time she got the president's phone call. Maybe now, she thought, she could uphold his legacy as a justice on the Court herself.

But the job of being a Supreme Court justice is so important that not even the president can just give it to someone. The United States Senate has to confirm the president's choice. And the Senate isn't easily convinced.

So Amy went to Capitol Hill, where the Senate sits, and answered questions from twenty-two senators. Their questions were very difficult: they asked about the Constitution, about her opinions and beliefs, and about her writings and experience.

They asked questions, and more questions, and more questions for four days straight. They definitely didn't make her life easy! The senators wanted to make absolutely sure she was the right person for the job.

Amy's answers were so sharp that, at one point, a senator asked if she was reading from her notes. So, she showed her notepad: it was completely blank. Her thoughts were so clear and well-organized in her head, she didn't need to write them down. Everyone was very impressed. Soon after, the Senate confirmed her nomination.

Hon. Amy Coney Barrett

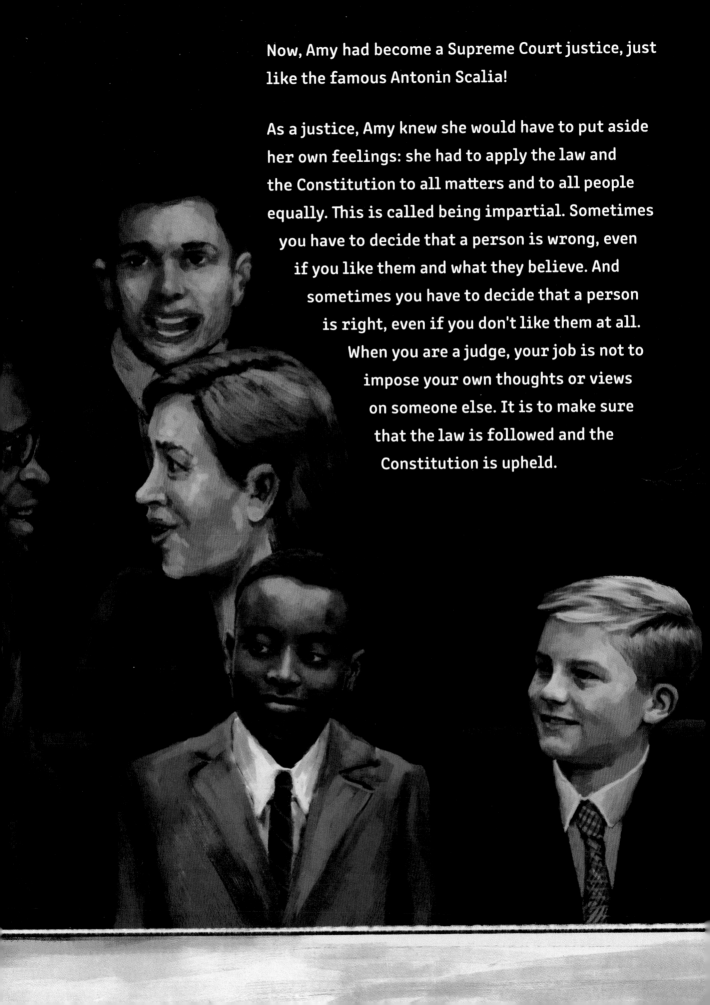

Now, Amy had become a Supreme Court justice, just like the famous Antonin Scalia!

As a justice, Amy knew she would have to put aside her own feelings: she had to apply the law and the Constitution to all matters and to all people equally. This is called being impartial. Sometimes you have to decide that a person is wrong, even if you like them and what they believe. And sometimes you have to decide that a person is right, even if you don't like them at all. When you are a judge, your job is not to impose your own thoughts or views on someone else. It is to make sure that the law is followed and the Constitution is upheld.

This is maybe the biggest difference between being a mother and being a judge. As a judge, you must treat everyone the same way: rich or poor, nice or mean, beautiful or ugly, smart or not so smart.

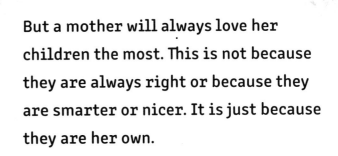

But a mother will always love her children the most. This is not because they are always right or because they are smarter or nicer. It is just because they are her own.

For Amy, being a mother is no less important than being a judge. Her children are lucky to have her as a mother, and we are lucky to have her as a Supreme Court justice. That's because she knows how to listen to her head and to her heart—and most importantly, when to listen to which.

INTERESTING FACTS ABOUT
Amy Coney Barrett

VIVIAN

HER FULL NAME IS AMY VIVIAN CONEY BARRETT.
VIVIAN IS ALSO THE NAME SHE AND JESSE GAVE
TO ONE OF THEIR DAUGHTERS.

✝

HER FAMILY IS CATHOLIC AND HER
FATHER WAS ORDAINED AS A DEACON.

SHE BELIEVES THAT OUR GREATEST IMPACT IN THE
WORLD IS THROUGH RAISING CHILDREN.

ΦΒΚ

IN COLLEGE, SHE BECAME A MEMBER OF THE
PHI BETA KAPPA SOCIETY, THE OLDEST ACADEMIC
HONOR SOCIETY IN THE UNITED STATES.

AS A LAWYER, SHE WAS A PART OF THE TEAM REPRESENTING
GEORGE W. BUSH IN THE BUSH V. GORE CASE, WHICH DECIDED
THE OUTCOME OF THE 2000 PRESIDENTIAL ELECTION.

450 OF AMY'S FORMER STUDENTS SIGNED
A LETTER TO THE UNITED STATES SENATE
COMMITTEE ON THE JUDICIARY IN SUPPORT OF
HER NOMINATION TO THE SUPREME COURT.

JUSTICE AMY CONEY BARRETT IS THE
FIFTH WOMAN TO SERVE ON THE UNITED
STATES SUPREME COURT.